TECHNOLOGY OF WAR

ROBIN CROSS

Wayland

TECHNOLOGY OF WAR

Other titles:

Aftermath of War
Children's War
Cities at War
Propaganda
Victims of War
Women and War
World Leaders

Cover illustration: A German submarine and a Dutch galleon sail towards Britain. The poster is Nazi propaganda aimed at reminding the Dutch of their attempt to invade England in 1673.
Contents page: A Spitfire over the skies of southern England.

First published in 1994 by
Wayland (Publishers) Ltd
61 Western Rd, Hove
East Sussex BN3 1JD, England

© Copyright 1994 Wayland (Publishers) Ltd

Series editor: Paul Mason
Book design: Mark Whitchurch

British Library Cataloguing in Publication Data
    Cross, Robin
    Technology of War-(Era of the Second World
    War Series)
    I.Title II.Series
    940.54

ISBN 0-7502-1160-1

Typeset by Mark Whitchurch
Printed and bound in Italy by Rotolito Lombarda
S.p.A.

Illustration acknowledgements
Thanks to John Yates, for drawing all maps and diagrams.
Thanks are extended also to the following, for allowing their photographs to be used in this book: Archiv fur Kunst und Geschichte, Berlin/Image Select cover, 5, 18, 22, 30, 37 bottom, 38; Camera Press 6, 17 both, 24, 34 bottom, 35, 44 top; Imperial War Museum 8, 10 bottom, 11, 14 bottom, 15, 23, 26, 29, 34, 37 top, 39; Popperfoto 4, 7, 10, 13, 31, 41, 42; Topham 16, 19, 20, 25, 27 bottom, 36, 40, 43, 44 bottom.

Contents

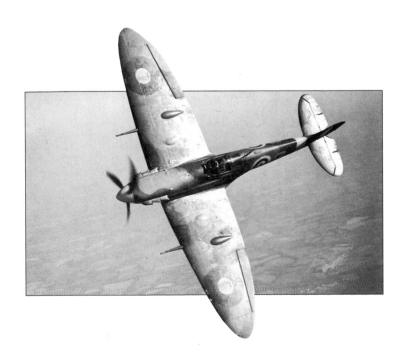

Introduction

From the chariot to the cruise missile the latest technology has always been harnessed to the waging of war. For much of this time the development of new weapons was relatively slow, but in the twentieth century - the age of atomic physics and the internal combustion engine - the pace was accelerated dramatically by two world wars.

These drew scientists and technicians into an increasingly close relationship with the military. In the Second World War (1939-45) scientists not only devised new weapons but also had an important say in determining how they were to be used in battle. The greater reliance on technology demanded large numbers of highly trained men and women to operate the new weapons. These people were as valuable as the weapons themselves. It cost more to train the crew of a four-engined heavy bomber than it did to build the bomber.

Many of the most important weapons of the Second World War had appeared in the First World War (1914-18). Aircraft and tanks had made an impact on the battlefield, but had not been decisive in the Allied defeat of Germany. The submarine, however, nearly won the First World War for Germany, just as it almost won the Second.

A German submarine during the First World War. Although submarines changed greatly between the wars, German U-boats threatened to cut Britain's supply lines to North America during both conflicts.

A Soviet poster compares the 1944 struggle against the German invasion with the 1917 revolution. It also shows the development of weapons, from bayonets and machine guns to huge tanks.

The years from 1918 to 1939 saw the development of the dominant technologies of the Second World War. Improved radio communications meant that warships at sea, large formations of tanks on land or aircraft overhead could be more easily controlled. The rapid expansion of the civil aviation industry, particularly in the USA, revolutionized aircraft design and performance. The biplanes of 1914-18 gave way to all-metal monoplanes with enclosed cockpits and retractable undercarriages. Engine power increased and the introduction of the supercharger boosted speed at high altitude.

Some of the key wartime technologies took a more roundabout route to their military application. Research into early forms of television in the 1920s produced the cathode ray tube, the most important component of the radar screens which, along with the RAF's Spitfire and Hurricane fighter planes, helped win the Battle of Britain. The radio navigation aids which had transformed civil aviation in the 1930s played an important part in the electronics war fought in the skies over England and Germany between 1940 and 1945. The most terrible weapon of all, the atomic bomb, was the fruit of peaceful research into the nature of the atom.

Spitfires and the Schneider Trophy

In the 1920s the international speed races for the Schneider Trophy gave a huge impetus to the design of fighter aircraft. The competing aircraft were so advanced that only governments could afford to pay for them and they were usually flown by highly experienced military pilots. British successes in this competition with the Supermarine seaplane pointed the way to the Supermarine Spitfire fighter, which entered service with the RAF in 1938 and remained in production throughout the Second World War.

The German Junkers Ju87 dive-bomber, one of the main weapons of blitzkrieg warfare. Combat-tested in the Spanish Civil War, the Stuka, as it was known, was a great success in the campaigns in Poland and France. It later proved vulnerable against British fighter aircraft, as it was virtually defenceless coming out of its dive. The Stuka was withdrawn from the Battle of Britain, but later used as a 'tank buster' in the USSR.

In the Spanish Civil War (1936-9) the Soviet Union and Germany tested their latest weapons, fighter planes, dive-bombers and tanks. Japan did the same in China, which it had invaded in 1937. These conflicts were dress rehearsals for the Second World War. The experiences gained in Spain and China enabled the Germans and the Japanese to combine new tactics and technology. Using them, they gained a series of rapid victories at the start of the Second World War.

By the summer of 1942 the technological tide had turned against the Axis (Germany, Japan and Italy). The weapons that had brought them victory were fast becoming obsolete. The Allies ranged against Germany and Japan possessed greater technical resources and were vastly stronger in numbers, raw materials and industrial muscle. After 1943 the new weapons introduced by Germany and Japan could prolong the war but could not prevent defeat.

In the Second World War each of the major fighting nations had its distinctive approach to technology. To offset their lack of personnel the British relied heavily on high technology. It has been estimated that up to one third of Britain's scientific talent and resources was consumed by the bombing offensive against Germany, which for most of the war was the only way Britain could strike directly at the heart of Germany.

Relentlessly squeezed between the huge war machines of the United States and the Soviet Union, Germany also used high technology, notably rockets and jet aircraft, as a means of staving off defeat. The Soviet Union, prepared to sustain heavy losses in battle, relied on basic, robust weapons which were easy to manufacture, use and maintain in the harsh conditions of the Eastern Front. The USA, on the other hand, placed great emphasis on the comfort and safety of its troops, and this was reflected in the major items of weaponry in which they flew, drove or sailed. The dropping of the atomic bomb on Japan was largely determined by American reluctance to suffer any more losses at the end of a long and bloody campaign. The atomic bomb was thus the ultimate technological weapon, which saved the conventional forces of the Allies the price of a victory paid for in their own blood.

Tank warfare

Until the autumn of 1942 the German army was the master of tank warfare. It was the inventor of *Blitzkrieg* (which means Lightning War), a method of waging war with rapid thrusts by large formations of tanks supported by aircraft, particularly dive-bombers. The Germans met a tough opponent in the Soviet Union's T-34 medium tank, perhaps the best all-round tank of the war. The T-34 was rugged, simple to manufacture, maintain and operate and well protected from enemy shells by its sloping forward armour. Its broad tracks enabled it to remain mobile in the heavy mud and thick snow of Russia. Its superb combination of speed, firepower and protection laid the foundation for all modern tank designs. From 1943 the T-34 was the mainstay of the new Soviet tank armies which tipped the balance on the Eastern Front against Germany.

The Soviet T-34 medium tank, the best all-round tank of the war. Nearly 50,000 were built during the war, and the T-34 continued in service with several armies until the 1960s.

Radar and the Battle of Britain

Two German Dornier 17 bombers above the Thames, near Woolwich Arsenal, on 7 September 1940. The Battle of Britain was raging over the skies of southern England at the time.

In Britain in the 1930s the ordinary citizen's view of air warfare was shaped by the warning given to the House of Commons in November 1932 by Prime Minister Stanley Baldwin: '*I think that it is well for the man in the street to realize that there is no power on earth that can protect him from being bombed. Whatever people may tell him, the bomber will always get through.*'[1]

Science was enlisted to defeat the bomber threat. At the beginning of 1935 the British government set up a Committee for the Scientific Survey of Air Defence. The committee began by exploring, and swiftly discarding, the possibility of a Death Ray to shoot down hostile aircraft. It realised that finding the enemy was the key to air defence.

Germany, France and the USA were also exploring the possibilities of radar, but only the British concentrated on its use in air defence. In 1937 the British Air Ministry began to build a line of Chain Home radar stations around Britain's east and south coasts.

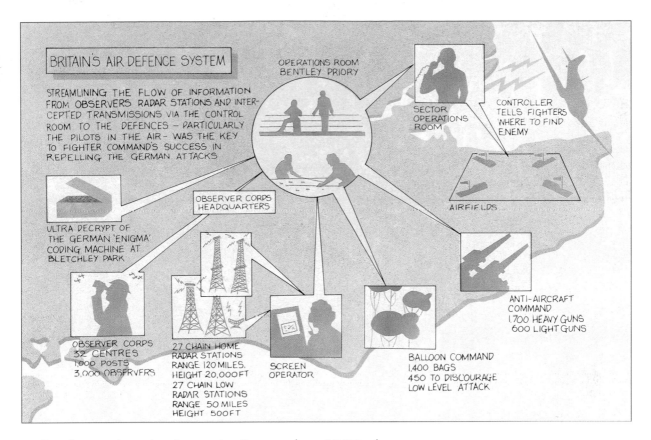

BRITAIN'S AIR DEFENCE SYSTEM

STREAMLINING THE FLOW OF INFORMATION FROM OBSERVERS RADAR STATIONS AND INTERCEPTED TRANSMISSIONS VIA THE CONTROL ROOM TO THE DEFENCES – PARTICULARLY THE PILOTS IN THE AIR – WAS THE KEY TO FIGHTER COMMAND'S SUCCESS IN REPELLING THE GERMAN ATTACKS

OPERATIONS ROOM BENTLEY PRIORY

SECTOR OPERATIONS ROOM

CONTROLLER TELLS FIGHTERS WHERE TO FIND ENEMY

OBSERVER CORPS HEADQUARTERS

AIRFIELDS

ULTRA DECRYPT OF THE GERMAN 'ENIGMA' CODING MACHINE AT BLETCHLEY PARK

OBSERVER CORPS 32 CENTRES 1,000 POSTS 3,000 OBSERVERS

27 CHAIN HOME RADAR STATIONS RANGE 120 MILES. HEIGHT 20,000 FT 27 CHAIN LOW RADAR STATIONS RANGE 50 MILES HEIGHT 500 FT

SCREEN OPERATOR

BALLOON COMMAND 1,400 BAGS 450 TO DISCOURAGE LOW LEVEL ATTACK

ANTI-AIRCRAFT COMMAND 1,700 HEAVY GUNS 600 LIGHT GUNS

By the outbreak of war, in September 1939, there were 20 such stations, stretching from Scotland to Land's End and easily identified by their tall latticed masts. By the spring of 1940 the system had been strengthened with Chain Home Low: radar that could pick up low-flying aircraft. Radar stations sent early warning of approaching *Luftwaffe* planes to Fighter Command in London. Information from radar stations and observer posts appeared on a huge chart of Britain. As planes moved, their symbols moved across the chart.

The Chain Home stations were only one part of an integrated air defence system covering the entire United Kingdom. It combined radar with coastal and inland observer posts, eight-gun fighter aircraft, anti-aircraft guns, searchlights and balloon barrages.

Radar played a vital role in the Battle of Britain (10 July - 31 October 1940) when only Fighter Command stood in the path of a German invasion of south-east England.

The value of radar
The value of radar to Fighter Command was summarised by the German fighter ace Adolf Galland, who fought in the Battle of Britain: 'In the battle we had to rely on our own human eyes. The British fighter pilots could depend on the radar eye, which was far more reliable and had a longer range. When we made contact with the enemy our briefings were already three hours old, [those of] the British . . . seconds old, the time it took to assess the latest position by means of radar to the transmission of attacking orders from Fighter Control to the already airborne force.'

Hawker Hurricanes of the Eagle Squadron of the RAF, flown by volunteers from the USA. The Hurricane was the RAF's first monoplane fighter, and could fly faster than 480kph.

The operations room at Duxford, a sector station during the Battle of Britain. The sector stations brought together information from radar stations and spotter posts, then passed it on to a central control room.

Using the Chain Home information, Fighter Command sent warnings and orders to its four Fighter Groups. Fighter squadrons 'scrambled' by Group orders were put into the air and guided by radio to their targets by controllers at the airfields, who plotted the enemy's position, altitude and course using information received from the radar network.

Without the warning radar gave, Fighter Command would have rapidly exhausted its reserves of pilots and aircraft flying around looking for the enemy. Radar enabled the fighters to remain on the ground until the enemy was known to be on his way and still take off in time to intercept him. This multiplied Fighter Command's strength many times over.

Although it was developing radar of its own, the *Luftwaffe* never grasped the importance of the Chain Home stations and the fighter control system to which they were linked. Attacks on the radar stations were abandoned early in the Battle of Britain, one of Germany's most serious errors of the war.

The war of the black boxes

The Battle of Britain was the first round in the radio and radar war for air supremacy fought by scientists and technicians on both sides. Rapid advances in technology made it easier for bombers to find their targets, particularly at night or in bad weather. But they also enabled the enemy's air defences to find and destroy the bombers. In turn, bombers were equipped with a range of new devices to frustrate enemy radars and night fighters. It was a see-saw battle in which each measure introduced by one side was met with a countermeasure devised by the other.

By the winter of 1940 the radio war was intensifying in the night skies over Britain. British ground controllers were using radar to guide night fighters towards German bombers. As the range narrowed between the fighter and the bomber, the fighter's own Airborne Interception Radar took over. During May 1941 improved techniques enabled British night fighters to claim 96 German bombers shot down.

A British Observer Corps post during the Battle of Britain. The post was in constant telephone contact with a reporting centre linked to clusters of observer posts.

11

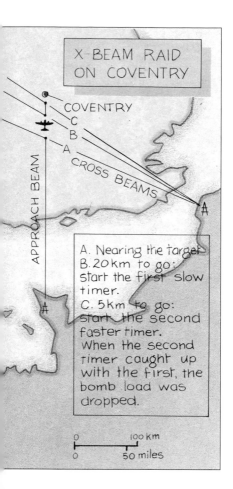

X-BEAM RAID ON COVENTRY

COVENTRY

C
B
A

CROSS BEAMS

APPROACH BEAM

A. Nearing the target.
B. 20 km to go:
start the first slow timer.
C. 5 km to go:
start the second faster timer.
When the second timer caught up with the first, the bomb load was dropped.

0   100 Km
|————————|
0   50 miles

Meanwhile, the *Luftwaffe* had been using radio beams to find important industrial targets in Britain. The first, adapted from a civilian blind-landing system introduced in the 1930s, was codenamed *Knickebein*, which is German for crooked leg. *Knickebein* employed two intersecting beams transmitted across England from France. The first, a mile wide at a range of 180 miles, kept the pilot on course with a steady, monotone signal. If he strayed out of the beam, the tone changed. The point at which the second beam crossed the first triggered a signal to release the bombs.

Knickebein was not an accurate system. At a range of 180 miles from the beam transmitters it gave the bomber crew only a 50 per cent chance of placing their bombs inside a one-kilometre diameter circle. Greater precision was achieved by the German X-system (see diagram). The X-system was used by specially trained 'pathfinding' crews. Their job was to go in first to mark the target with flares and incendiary bombs for the following waves of bombers.

The disadvantage of the German beams was that they were vulnerable to radio countermeasures. The British quickly discovered and jammed *Knickebein* and the X-system. This reduced the accuracy of German bombing and helped radar-controlled anti-aircraft guns and night fighters to shoot down bombers compelled to fly on bright moonlit nights to find their targets.

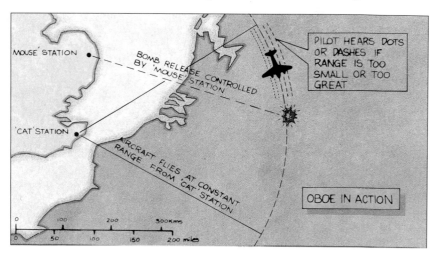

MOUSE STATION

BOMB RELEASE CONTROLLED BY 'MOUSE' STATION

PILOT HEARS DOTS OR DASHES IF RANGE IS TOO SMALL OR TOO GREAT

'CAT' STATION

AIRCRAFT FLIES AT CONSTANT RANGE FROM 'CAT' STATION

OBOE IN ACTION

0   100   200   300Kms
|——|——|——|——|
0   50   100   150   200 miles

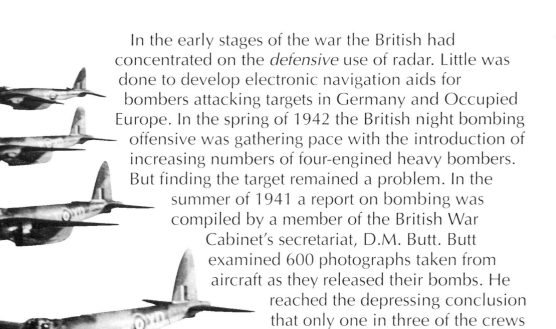

In the early stages of the war the British had concentrated on the *defensive* use of radar. Little was done to develop electronic navigation aids for bombers attacking targets in Germany and Occupied Europe. In the spring of 1942 the British night bombing offensive was gathering pace with the introduction of increasing numbers of four-engined heavy bombers. But finding the target remained a problem. In the summer of 1941 a report on bombing was compiled by a member of the British War Cabinet's secretariat, D.M. Butt. Butt examined 600 photographs taken from aircraft as they released their bombs. He reached the depressing conclusion that only one in three of the crews who were thought to have bombed their targets had actually got within 8 kilometres of them. On nights when there was no moon the figures fell to one in fifteen.

The versatile Mosquito, built of wood to save scarce light alloys. It served as a fighter, bomber, ground-attack and photo-reconaissance aircraft. It was Mosquitos that used Oboe to guide them to their targets.

The first British radio aid to navigation, codenamed Gee, was introduced in the winter of 1941. Gee enabled a bomber's navigator to fix his position by reference to radio pulses transmitted from three stations in England. Like the X-system, Gee proved simple to jam, and by the end of 1942 it had come to the end of its useful life.

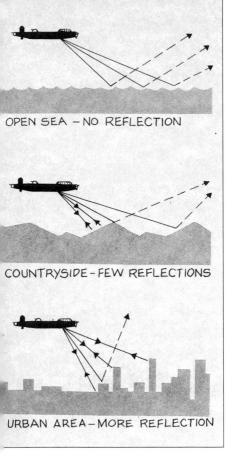

OPEN SEA – NO REFLECTION

COUNTRYSIDE – FEW REFLECTIONS

URBAN AREA – MORE REFLECTION

How H2S worked: radar signals from the aircraft were reflected back in progressively greater amounts by water, countryside and cities. This enabled the aircraft's navigator to build up a picture of the ground below.

A captured German Junkers Ju88 night fighter with a nose array of SN-2 radar. These fighters also had equipment that enabled them to home in on the H2S signals of British bombers.

Oboe, introduced in the winter of 1942, was a blind-bombing system that could achieve accuracies of 180 metres. The Oboe system was difficult to jam, but its range was limited by the curve of the earth to about 450 kilometres, although this took in most of the German industrial region of the Ruhr. In its early version Oboe could handle only one aircraft at a time on its bombing run. As a result it was used only in the high-altitude Mosquito bombers of RAF Bomber Command's Pathfinder Force. Their task was to deliver incendiary devices that caused fires for the main force of heavy bombers to aim at.

What was needed was a system that was independent of control by ground stations. The answer was the H2S, which went into service early in 1943. H2S was an advanced downward-looking radar, housed in the bomber's belly, which scanned the ground below. The returning echoes, displayed on a cathode ray tube known as a Plan Position Indicator, gave a continuous picture of the terrain over which the aircraft was flying.

As the German air defences became more dependent on radar and radio, the British devoted more time and effort to jamming them. In 1942 Allied bombers were equipped with transmitters that radiated noise on the frequency of German early-warning radar.

Later electronic measures included Jostle, a communications jammer which sent a loud, raucous noise on the wavelengths used by German fighter control channels. Bomber Command's most spectacular jamming success was achieved on the night of 24 July 1943, during a big raid on Hamburg. The city's radar-controlled air defences were thrown into chaos when the British bombers released clouds of aluminium foil strips called Window, each of which was cut to half the wavelength of the German radars. Window gave the appearance of many false targets on the radar. When dropped in huge quantities, it could blot out German radar screens altogether. It took the Germans a year to develop an airborne radar, SN-2, which was not affected by Window. Nevertheless, Window was used to the end of the war by the British and Americans (who called it Chaff). By the end of the war American bombers based in Britain and flying against Germany by day were using up about 2,000 tonnes of Chaff a month.

A bombed German city, Dresden. The approach of Allied bombers was sometimes disguised by Window.

In November 1943 Bomber Command formed 100 Group, whose sole purpose was to use radar and radio countermeasures against Germany's night defences. Towards the end of the war 100 Group could put up as many as 90 jamming aircraft in a big operation, using them in different combinations to keep the enemy guessing. It has been estimated that jamming saved the RAF as many as 1,000 bombers and their crews from the beginning of 1943 to the end of the war. Attacking by day, US bombers presented easier targets for German fighters and anti-aircraft guns, which did not have to rely so heavily on the extra eye provided by radar. But jamming still proved its worth, saving as many as 400 US bombers and their crews.

Dropping Window over Hamburg

'Our bomb aimer dropped the Window out of a trap in the underside of the nose. When this was opened, we had an almighty draught straight back down the fuselage and most of the Window seemed to be blowing back into the aeroplane, instead of dropping clear. I have a vivid mental picture of sitting in the wireless position with just a glow of a tiny lamp on the set and watching a steady stream of these little strips going past me and disappearing into the darkness over the main spar, a bit like watching a shoal of river fish darting along in murky water.' Pilot Officer R. Clarke, 12 Squadron, RAF Bomber Command.

The Battle of the Atlantic

Britain's wartime Prime Minister, Winston Churchill, considered that the Battle of the Atlantic was the `dominating factor all through the war. Never could we forget that everything depended on its outcome.' Without the supplies that reached Britain from North America, the British would have been unable to continue the war. For the British the Battle of the Atlantic was the longest campaign of the war, fought from the very first day to the last.

In the First World War, German submarines, known as U-boats, came close to starving Britain into surrender by cutting its supply line to America. In the Second World War they once again came close to victory, but at the height of the battle were defeated by Allied technology.

In many ways the technological problems posed by the Battle of the Atlantic resembled those in the air war. To defeat the U-boats the Allies needed the equipment to detect and destroy them in huge expanses of ocean. Until 1943, however, Allied equipment was inadequate. The radar sets installed in convoy escorts in 1940 could only detect submarines at short range. Equally unreliable was sonar, the sound equivalent of radar, which detected a submerged submarine by bouncing a sound signal off its hull. Sonar readings were often distorted by wrecks, shoals of fish and changes in underwater temperature.

A look-out keeps watch from a German U-boat. U-boats were at their most vulnerable when surfaced.

At first the U-boats gained the upper hand. Hunting in groups known as wolfpacks and guided to their targets by German long-range reconnaissance aircraft, the U-boats could stay at sea for long periods, refuelled by supply submarines known as milch cows. By coordinating surface torpedo attacks at night they could often overwhelm the convoy escorts by sheer weight of numbers.

The Battle of the Atlantic reached crisis point for the Allies at the beginning of 1943. U-boats sank 203,000 tonnes of shipping in January, 359,000 tonnes in February and 627,000 tonnes in March. Ships were being sunk at twice the rate they were being built, while for every U-boat sunk two were launched. Britain's food, fuel and munitions lifeline, stretching across the Atlantic from the United States, was in danger of being cut. Admiral Dönitz, the commander of the German navy, believed that he had victory within his grasp.

At this point science began to work in favour of the Allies. The most important technical breakthrough came with the development of a powerful new centimetric radar based on a British invention, the cavity magnetron valve. The accuracy of centimetric radar was demonstrated in April 1941 when it detected a surfaced submarine at a range of ten miles and a periscope at 1,200 metres. It was immediately clear that long-range patrol aircraft equipped with centimetric radar would be a deadly threat to U-boats.

The radar could not be rushed into service overnight. Sets had to be designed which did not create radio interference; production had to be organized; and crews trained to use it. Above all, the secret of the cavity magnetron had to be kept from the Germans in case they found a way to jam it.

The captain and crew of a U-boat relax in the sun during the Battle of the Atlantic. In the summer of 1942 the average life of a U-boat was 13 months: by 1945 it had fallen to only three months.

The German battleship Bismark sinks the British battleship Hood, 24 May 1941. The Bismark was hunted down by the Royal Navy and sunk three days later, after her steering had been jammed by a torpedo bomber from the aircraft carrier Ark Royal.

In the spring of 1943 air-to-surface (ASV) radar was introduced in the Battle of the Atlantic. Its effect was immediate. Aircraft equipped with ASV, searchlights and depth charges were able to detect and kill surfaced U-boats during the hours of darkness. In May 1943 aircraft accounted for 22 of the 36 U-boats sunk by the Allies.

For some time the Germans were convinced that these submarine losses were the result of a new infra-red device carried by the aircraft. In fact this was a clever hoax. Eventually the Germans retrieved a cavity magnetron from a radar set in a crashed British bomber (the device was practically indestructible) and unpicked its secrets. U-boats were fitted with an antenna which picked up centimetric radar transmissions at a range of up to 15 kilometres which often gave the submarines time to dive. Later antennae gave warnings at a range of about 45 kilometres.

Nevertheless, U-boat losses continued to mount. By mid-summer 1943 centimetric radar was one of a number of new measures that were steadily crippling the U-boats. High Frequency Direction Finding (known as Huff-Duff) enabled escorts to pinpoint and shadow U-boats when they were transmitting signals back to base. American Very Long Range (VLR) B-24 Liberator bombers closed the gap in the mid-Atlantic in which U-boats had operated free from air attack. Hunter-killer support groups built around fast escort aircraft carriers took a heavy toll of U-boats.

In August 1943 the tonnage of Allied shipping launched overtook that lost to U-boats for the first time in the war. Admiral Dönitz was forced to concede defeat, but the German navy did not give up the struggle.

The U-boat's biggest weakness was its need to surface in order to recharge its batteries. Improved Allied detection methods meant that the long periods of time spent on the surface were becoming increasingly dangerous. It was vital to improve underwater endurance and speed. The first solution was the Schnorkel tube, which was clipped to the U-boat's conning tower when it dived and enabled it to run submerged while recharging its batteries. Meanwhile new types of submarine were being developed. The ocean-going Type XXI U-boat, the ancestor of all modern submarines, used very powerful batteries and a streamlined hull to give it an underwater range of up to 500 kilometres. Had it been introduced in large numbers earlier in the war, the Type XXI might have turned the tide in the Battle of the Atlantic. In a relatively calm sea it could outpace an attacker while remaining submerged. Its high underwater speed meant that it could manoeuvre and attack entirely submerged, and it could dive much deeper than other U-boats, manoeuvring more violently as it did so. The Type XXI was a formidable weapon but only a handful saw active service before the war ended.

A US Liberator bomber in RAF markings. Liberators were deadly submarine hunters. From 1943 they carried acoustic torpedoes which homed in on the sound of a U-boat's propellors. 'It's no longer any fun to sail in a U-boat. We don't really mind even a cruiser, and we can face destroyers without turning a hair. But if an aircraft is there, we've had it. It directs surface craft to the spot even if it does not attack itself.' (A captured officer from the U 506, sunk in the North Atlantic, 12 July 1943.)

Mass production

In the early years of this century the British statesman Sir Edward Grey likened the economy of the United States to a gigantic boiler. *'Once the fire is lighted under it, there is no limit to the power it can generate.'*

The fire was lit under the US economy on 7 December 1941, when the Japanese launched a surprise attack on the great American naval base at Pearl Harbor on the Hawaiian island of Oahu. The next day the USA declared war on Japan. Three days later Germany and Italy, honouring treaty obligations with Japan, declared war on the United States. The British Prime Minister, Winston Churchill, instantly recognized that this was a turning point in the war. As soon as the economic might of the United States was fully engaged against Germany and Japan, Churchill's first thought was *'we have won the war.'*

From March 1941 the United States had been supplying the British with weapons and war materials under the terms of the Lend-Lease Act. After the Japanese attack on Pearl Harbor the aid was extended to the USSR. Over the next three years the USA provided its allies with civil and military aid sufficient for them to equip 2,000 infantry divisions. The key to victory in Europe and the Pacific lay in the sheer size and efficiency of the American economy, which applied the latest business methods to war production and the massive expansion of the US armed forces.

The US way of waging war, backed up by industrial might. Landing ships bring a steady flow of supplies to the US beachhead on the Pacific island of Okinawa.

In 1939 the United States manufactured only a small amount of military equipment for its own needs. By 1944 it was producing no less than 40 per cent of the world's armaments. In 1940 only 346 tanks had been built in the USA; in 1944 alone 17,500 rolled off the production lines. Figures for aircraft production leapt from 2,141 in 1940 to 96,318 in 1944.

American material and human resources seemed almost limitless. One wartime Ford motor plant alone employed 42,000 people. Much of their output was destined for the Soviet Union, which by 1945 had taken delivery of nearly 500,000 US-made trucks and jeeps. Red Army soldiers advanced on Berlin in American trucks or marched westward in American boots, 15 million pairs of which were supplied to the Soviet Union. Soviet war production was boosted by US machine tools, high-grade petroleum, steel, copper and rail locomotives and track. US shipyards supplied the answer to heavy merchant shipping losses during the Battle of the Atlantic. It came in the form of 3,000 Liberty Ships, general-purpose freighters whose average construction time was only 42 days. On one occasion a Liberty Ship was built in only five days.

The amphibious tactics used by the USA to capture the Pacific island of Tarawa in November 1943. Later the USA increased the initial 'softening up' bombardment to smash the enemy's heavily fortified defences. Communications between ships and ashore were improved, so that fire could be quickly directed against specific targets.

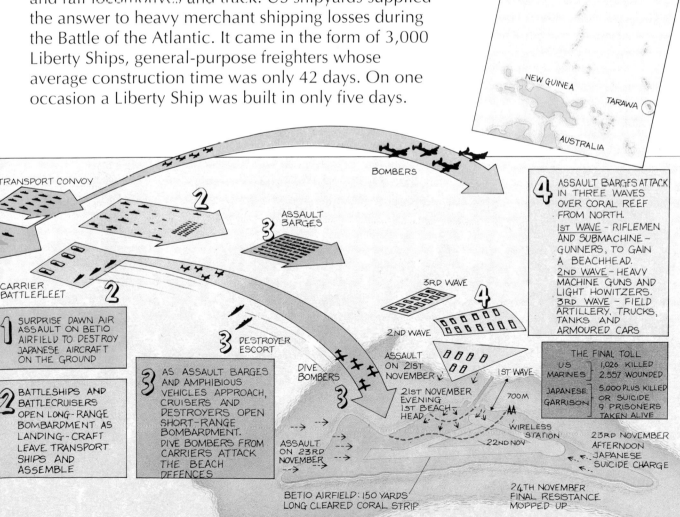

JAPAN

NEW GUINEA

TARAWA

AUSTRALIA

TRANSPORT CONVOY

BOMBERS

ASSAULT BARGES

CARRIER BATTLEFLEET

4 ASSAULT BARGES ATTACK IN THREE WAVES OVER CORAL REEF FROM NORTH.
1ST WAVE – RIFLEMEN AND SUBMACHINE-GUNNERS, TO GAIN A BEACHHEAD.
2ND WAVE – HEAVY MACHINE GUNS AND LIGHT HOWITZERS.
3RD WAVE – FIELD ARTILLERY, TRUCKS, TANKS AND ARMOURED CARS

3RD WAVE

2ND WAVE

1 SURPRISE DAWN AIR ASSAULT ON BETIO AIRFIELD TO DESTROY JAPANESE AIRCRAFT ON THE GROUND

2 BATTLESHIPS AND BATTLECRUISERS OPEN LONG-RANGE BOMBARDMENT AS LANDING-CRAFT LEAVE TRANSPORT SHIPS AND ASSEMBLE

3 DESTROYER ESCORT

3 AS ASSAULT BARGES AND AMPHIBIOUS VEHICLES APPROACH, CRUISERS AND DESTROYERS OPEN SHORT-RANGE BOMBARDMENT. DIVE BOMBERS FROM CARRIERS ATTACK THE BEACH DEFENCES

DIVE BOMBERS

ASSAULT ON 21ST NOVEMBER

21ST NOVEMBER EVENING 1ST BEACH-HEAD

1ST WAVE

700M

AA

WIRELESS STATION

22ND NOV

ASSAULT ON 23RD NOVEMBER

THE FINAL TOLL

US MARINES	1,026 KILLED	2,557 WOUNDED
JAPANESE GARRISON	5,000 PLUS KILLED OR SUICIDE	9 PRISONERS TAKEN ALIVE

23RD NOVEMBER AFTERNOON JAPANESE SUICIDE CHARGE

24TH NOVEMBER FINAL RESISTANCE MOPPED UP

BETIO AIRFIELD: 150 YARDS LONG CLEARED CORAL STRIP

The Liberty Ships served in the Atlantic, the Mediterranean and the Pacific. The Americans combined technology and technique to fight a new kind of war based on the aircraft carrier. In the First World War (1914-18) battleships had ruled the seas, slugging it out over ranges of up to 18,000 metres. In the vast expanses of the Pacific Ocean, however, the most important ship was the aircraft carrier, whose dive-bombers and torpedo-bombers could strike at an enemy hundreds of kilometres away. At the time of Pearl Harbor the USA had three carriers in the Pacific and the Japanese eleven. Japanese naval superiority did not last long. Japan never recovered from the loss of its main carrier fleet at the Battle of Midway in June 1942, the first naval battle in which the main opposing ships never saw each other.

By mid-1944 all 15 of the Japanese carriers brought into service since 1941 had been sunk or put out of action by the US Navy. Of the 27 fleet carriers added to the US Navy only one had been sunk. The Americans built special fast carrier task forces around their Essex-class fleet carriers, which entered service in 1942 and could carry up to 100 aircraft. The American carriers' radar (the Japanese had none) gave them coverage extending out for 160 kilometres and aided control of their own aircraft, which remained in radio contact with the mother ships at all times.

A US Grumman F6F-3 Hellcat ablaze on the deck of an aircraft carrier. During the Battle of Midway (June 1942) Japan's carrier fleet was all but destroyed, giving the USA supremacy in the Pacific War.

Only 15 per cent of the total US war effort was devoted to the Pacific, but once it had hit its stride the Japanese were always going to be outgunned. American submarines tightened the grip on Japan by sinking the shipping on which Japanese war industry depended for its oil and raw materials. By the end of the war nearly 60 per cent of all the merchant shipping lost by the Japanese had been sunk by American submarines. And this in spite of the fact that one in every three of the US torpedoes was defective.

American fast carrier task forces provided air cover for the US amphibious forces as they leapfrogged across the Pacific, using islands as stepping stones in the advance on Japan. For these complex, large-scale operations a new family of tracked, armoured landing craft (called amtracs) was developed. Their task was to drive ashore and across heavily defended beaches before disembarking the troops they carried. By the end of the war the United States had produced nearly 19,000 tracked landing vehicles, many of which had the turret and gun of a light tank.

Heavy though the fighting was in the Pacific, the US combat troops in the front line were greatly outnumbered by those responsible for keeping them supplied. Huge airfields and bases were needed to support the Pacific drive. Long-range landing operations were made possible by the huge `fleet trains' of ships which replenished the US armadas at sea with immense quantities of ammunition, fuel and food. This was war fought on a colossal scale, in which US technology and sheer weight of industrial production were combined in an irresistible force.

Victory through air power – the B29

Designed in 1941 and introduced to combat in 1944, the Boeing B-29 Superfortress heavy bomber (shown above) was the symbol of American military might. It could fly over greater distances, and with a heavier load, than any other aircraft then in existence. It was used exclusively in the Pacific where B-29s had to fly well over 1,600 kilometres and back to bomb the home islands of Japan. The B-29's advanced technology included pressurisation in the nose and parts of the fuselage, and remote-controlled gun turrets. Cruising at 220mph, it could carry 5,000lb of bombs over a range of 5,230 kilometres or a maximum of 20,000lb of bombs over short ranges.

D-Day

On 6 June 1944 the invasion of Normandy, in north-west France, was launched by the Allies. Codenamed Overlord, it was the greatest amphibious operation in history. By midnight on 6 June over 150,000 US, British and Canadian troops had been landed in France by sea and air.

Never before had a major military operation involved so much scientific preparation and invention. At every level in the planning and mounting of Overlord scientists played an important part. By this stage in the war they were able to analyze battlefield experience to devise new weapons and tactics, and improve existing ones, to meet the challenge presented by Overlord.

A Sherman Firefly tank, armed with a British 17-pound gun, comes ashore in Normandy during Operation Overlord, the Allied invasion of northern France.

Nothing was left to chance. The invasion beaches were chosen only after extensive analysis of sand samples brought back from Normandy by special commando units. Every inch of the invasion area was photographed by Allied reconnaissance aircraft. Sir Solly Zuckerman, chief scientific adviser to the Allied invasion force, studied the results of the photographic missions to devise the Transportation Plan that preceded Overlord. This was a scheme for Allied bombers to destroy the railway systems in western Germany and France which the Germans would use to reinforce their troops in Normandy after the Allies came ashore. A quick German reinforcement might have spelled disaster for the Allies in the first week of the invasion.

US troops wade ashore in Normandy, 6 June 1944, during the first days of Overlord.

The Transportation Plan went ahead after a trial air raid on 6 March 1944 in which Oboe-guided Pathfinders successfully attacked rail yards at Trappes near Paris. In the weeks leading up to Overlord nearly 80,000 tonnes of bombs fell on railway targets, severely limiting the Germans' ability to hit the Allies with a swift and powerful attack after the Normandy landings.

Less dramatic but equally essential to the success of Overlord on 6 June was the continuous supply of accurate weather reports. Although weather conditions in the early days of June 1944 were very poor, a window of fair weather was predicted to start on 6 June and last for several days. It was on this advice that the decision was made to launch Overlord on 6 June.

A Sherman flail tank (on the right) which could clear a lane three metres wide through a minefield at a speed of about 2 kilometres an hour.

As the Allied armada of 5,000 ships headed across the Channel, an electronic deception operation was mounted to reinforce the long-held German belief that the invasion, when it came, would be in the Pas de Calais rather than Normandy. Naval launches headed towards Calais and Boulogne. Each towed balloons fitted with special reflectors that produced radar echoes similar to those made by large troop ships. Overhead bombers dropped streams of Window, creating more false radar signals. This phantom invasion force convinced German radar operators that huge air and sea fleets were making for the Pas de Calais. Even after the Allies had landed in Normandy, the Germans clung to the belief that this was just a feint attack to be followed by the main blow against the Pas de Calais. As a result they held back strong forces in the Pas de Calais which might have tipped the balance in Normandy.

Once the Allied troops were ashore, some kind of port would be needed to bring in supplies and ammunition. In case a harbour in working order could not be captured, the Allies decided to create two artificial harbours off the Normandy landing area, one to service the American beaches and the other to supply the British. The prefabricated parts of these harbours would be towed across the English Channel and fitted together after the first landings.

Weapons of invasion

To clear a way through minefield and beach obstacles, and punch holes in sea walls, the Allies developed a range of ingenious weapons. Special landing craft were fitted with rocket batteries known as Grasshoppers. When close to the beach, the Grasshoppers fired a 60-second salvo which could blast a path up the beach 110 metres long and eight metres wide. Tanks and armoured engineers needed to get ashore quickly to deal with the obstacles that remained and to provide support for the infantry coming ashore. Duplex Drive (DD) swimming tanks, which had propellers and canvas skirts to keep them afloat, were launched offshore. Once ashore, the DDs fought alongside special armoured assault teams called 'funnies', which had been developed by Major-General Percy Hobart, commander of the British 79th Armoured Division. Hobart's 'funnies' included modified Sherman tanks called Crabs, equipped with a large flail at the front. The flail beat the ground to set off land mines. The Bobbin was a converted Churchill tank carrying a large device resembling a huge cotton reel which unrolled matting to provide a track across soft sand. The Crocodile was a flame-throwing Churchill that carried its fuel on a trailer towed by the tank.

Codenamed Mulberries, the artificial harbours consisted of a breakwater and an outer wall constructed two miles offshore by sinking ships and vast caissons, hollow floating concrete blocks, some of which were the size of five-storey buildings. This created an area of calm water inside which piers were built and connected to the shore by floating roadways made of sections of articulated steel. The construction of the Mulberries consumed two million tonnes of steel and concrete. It required every tugboat in the United Kingdom plus many more from the United States to tow the sections of the Mulberries across the English Channel.

A DUKW amphibious vehicle in action off the coast of Normandy. The Duck, as it was known, was a floating truck with a propeller capable of carrying a two-ton load.

The return of bad weather limited the usefulness of the Mulberries. Between 18 and 22 June the artificial harbours were battered by heavy seas. The British Mulberry rode out the storm but the American Mulberry at Arromanches was badly broken up. In the end the Americans were landing more supplies across open beaches than were arriving at the repaired British Mulberry.

More successful was Pluto (Pipeline under the Ocean) which ensured a continuous supply of petrol from England to France. The Pluto pipeline was unrolled off 15-metre drums like sheathed telephone cable and laid on the sea bottom as the drum was pulled along by a tug.

Tugs tow Phoenix breakwaters, major components of the Mulberry harbours the Allies used during Overlord, as part of the build-up to D-day.

Codes and computers

One of the greatest Allied technical triumphs of the Second World War was won not on the battlefield but in the Buckinghamshire countryside at Bletchley Park, the home of the British Government Code and Cypher School.

It was at Bletchley Park that the British deciphered the top secret German signals encoded on the Enigma machine. The Enigma machine had been invented and marketed in 1923 by a German, Arthur Scherbius. He saw the machine as a way of keeping business correspondence secret, but the German armed forces quickly spotted its military potential. By 1935 Enigma was being used as standard equipment by all branches of the German armed forces and intelligence departments.

The first modern computer

Some top secret German communications were made not by Enigma but a machine cypher known to the Allies as Fish which included more security safeguards than Enigma. Two Fish machines were captured in North Africa in May 1943. To deal with Fish the British built a primitive but effective semi-electronic computer codenamed Colossus, which started work at Bletchley in December 1943. By February 1944 Colossus could read Fish messages within hours. Its successor, Colossus II, which went into service in June 1944, had a limited memory and was the world's first programmed electronic digital computer.

The Enigma machine looked like a cross between a portable typewriter and a cash register. Inside the machine was a complex system of gears, electric wiring and a series of drums. Each of the drums carried an alphabet on the outside. Any letter typed by the Enigma operator on the keyboard could be transposed into an infinite variety of different letters. When A was struck on the keyboard it might be transposed to M. When M was struck on an Enigma deciphering machine after receiving the message, it would be transposed back to A. The machines were often altered so that different letters came out to represent A. So long as both machines were altered at the same time the system continued to work. Encoded messages, seemingly random groups of letters, were sent in Morse code, protecting German radio communications from eavesdroppers. The Germans were convinced that the Enigma code was unbreakable.

In the 1930s early forms of the Enigma code were broken by a team working for Poland's military intelligence. Before the outbreak of war in September 1939, the Poles shared their knowledge with the British and presented them with an Enigma machine. Mathematicians at Bletchley Park immediately began working on the later, modified Enigma codes that had defeated the Poles. By the end of the war there were 10,000 people at Bletchley, housed in a hotchpotch of temporary accommodation built in the grounds. It was a very British organization, full of brilliant eccentrics and misfits, but it worked.

Knowing how the Enigma machine worked was not enough. It was vital to discover the Enigma keys, the settings that were changed three times a day. There was no shortage of raw material on which to work. Using extra-sensitive US-built receivers, the Y-Service, a top secret British radio interception network, listened in to the apparently meaningless groups of letters encoded by Enigma and transmitted in Morse code. They were taken down and then sent to Bletchley, where the Enigma secret was unlocked.

The German General Heinz Guderian in his armoured command vehicle in France in 1940. In the foreground is a German Enigma code machine with three wheels and a typewriter keyboard.

The US battleship West Virginia ablaze after the Japanese attack on Pearl Harbour, 7 December 1941. Although the US forces were able to read the Japanese naval codes, the attack was a surprise because the Japanese had kept radio silence.

The principal weapons used by the British decoders were electromechanical computers, nicknamed Bronze Goddesses, which were matched to the electric wiring of the Enigma machine. Eventually many Enigma signals were being read at the same speed by the British as by the Germans.

Information from the deciphered Enigma signals was codenamed Ultra. It ranged from routine orders to detailed plans for major battles. Ultra was surrounded by the greatest secrecy to prevent the Germans discovering that the code had been broken. The British shared Ultra with the Americans but not with their Soviet allies, although they sometimes provided the Soviets with information based on Ultra. The Germans never realized that their codes had been broken.

The USA, too, had expert codebreakers. Long before the USA entered the war in December 1941, they had broken both the Japanese JN25b naval code and Purple, an incredibly complicated Japanese machine cipher used for diplomatic communications. It took two years to break Purple. Information from the Japanese codes was distributed under the codename Magic.

What contribution did Ultra and Magic make to Allied victory? There are limits to the effectiveness of even the best intelligence. At the beginning of December 1941 the US forces were alert to the possibility of a Japanese attack in the Pacific. But by maintaining absolute radio silence and hiding their aircraft carriers in the vastness of the Pacific, the Japanese achieved complete surprise when on 7 December they attacked the US naval base at Pearl Harbor. In May 1941 Ultra was used to provide the British commander on the island of Crete, General Freyburg, with details of imminent German parachute landings. But Freyburg lacked the troops and transport to launch decisive attacks at the danger points when the paratroops landed. He lost the battle for Crete.

In contrast, Magic played a vital part at Midway (June 1942), the decisive naval battle in the Pacific. It enabled the US Navy to position its carrier fleet to defeat a much stronger Japanese force. In April 1943 intercepted Japanese signals also made it possible for US fighter aircraft to shoot down and kill Admiral Yamamoto, commander of the Combined Fleet, while he was flying on a tour of inspection in the western Pacific. With Yamamoto's death the Japanese lost their best commander.

Admiral Yamamoto, commander of the Japanese fleet, whose plane was shot down by US fighters acting on Magic information, from decoded Japanese messages.

Columns of oily smoke pour from a torpedoed oil tanker, 9 October 1942.

Ultra came into its own during and after the Normandy landings in 1944, when time and many lives were saved by Allied foreknowledge of German plans and positions. Winston Churchill called the decoding teams at Bletchley 'the geese which laid the golden eggs but which never cackled.' The secret of Ultra was not revealed until the early 1970s.

Hitler's revenge weapons

In the small hours of Tuesday, 13 June 1944, a small pilotless aircraft with a wingspan of 5 metres flew from France to England. Crossing the English coast at a speed of about 650kph, it continued toward London, making a swishing sound and sending a jet of flaming exhaust from its rear. As it passed overhead the sound it made changed to a chugging which one observer likened to a Model-T Ford automobile climbing a steep hill. A few minutes later, at 4.20am, the sinister aircraft's engine cut out. There was a short silence and then it plunged to earth near the village of Swanscombe, 30 kilometres east of central London. There was a huge explosion but no casualties. The first of Adolf Hitler's Vergeltungswaffen (meaning Revenge Weapons), or V-weapons, had arrived in England.

Searchlights sweep the sky in a war artist's impression of a V-1 flying bomb attack on London in 1944.

V-1s discovered by US troops in an underground factory at Nordhausen in Germany on 10 April 1945. 32,000 V-1s were produced. Allied bombing raids on the launching sites held up the flying bomb offensive, but it was the overrunning of the sites by Allied armies that brought the campaign to an end.

The story of Germany's pilotless weapons programme began in the late 1920s when a 19 year old student at the Berlin Technical College, Wernher von Braun, joined the German Amateur Rocket Society. The Society built experimental missiles which greatly impressed a German artillery officer, Walter Dornberger. Von Braun and Dornberger began to work together to produce a big, transportable military rocket. This was to be a substitute for the conventional long range artillery forbidden to the German Army by the Versailles Treaty signed by a defeated Germany after the First World War.

Funded by the German Army, Dornberger established an experimental station at Peenemünde on a remote island in the Baltic Sea. By the summer of 1942 Dornberger was ready for a test firing of von Braun's A-4 rocket, which was to become known to the Allies at the V-2.

Meanwhile the *Luftwaffe* had developed a pilotless weapon of its own. Near Peenemünde it was preparing to test its FZG-76 flying bomb, the V-1. The V-1 had a number of important advantages over its big rocket rival. It was cheap and easy to produce and burned low-grade petrol instead of the scarce liquid oxygen and high-grade alcohol needed to power the V-2. Unknown to the Germans the British had got wind of the V-weapon programme. On the night of 17/18 August 1943 nearly 600 heavy bombers pounded the plant at Peenemünde, setting back the V-2 programme by at least two months.

The Germans planned to begin the V-weapon campaign by hitting London with 500 V-1s a day,

Before: an RAF photo of the German rocket research plant at Peenemunde.

making the city uninhabitable. Once again Allied bombers intervened. From December 1943 they dropped thousands of tonnes of bombs on the conspicuous concrete and steel ramps built to launch V-1s from sites in northern France. The V-weapon offensive did not get under way until a week after the Allied invasion of north-west Europe on D-Day, 6 June 1944.

The doodlebugs, as the V-1s were quickly dubbed, thrust Londoners back into the front line for the first time since the Blitz (the German bombing offensive against London which lasted from September 1940 to May 1941). The V-1s were not particularly accurate, but London was a very big target and the Germans intended the effect of the flying bombs to be indiscriminate. By the end of August 1944 approximately 21,000 people in the London region had been killed or seriously injured by doodlebugs. Nearly a million houses had been damaged, many of them beyond repair. At the start of the V-1 campaign the British government evacuated 250,000 mothers and young children from London. Over a million more people left the city of their own accord. At night thousands sheltered in the London Underground stations, as they had done during the Blitz.

What made the V-1 particularly terrifying was the fact that it could clearly be heard approaching. When the doodlebug's guidance system told the motor to stop there was 15 seconds' silence before it plunged to earth to explode with a force that could destroy a whole city block. If the engine cut out after the V-1 had flown overhead, you were safe. If not, the 15 seconds of silence might be your last.

After: a picture of Peenemunde after the RAF bombing raid of 17/18 August 1943. Two of the rocket programme's top scientists were among the 735 killed in the raid. The Peenemunde raid was the only time in the war that the full power of Bomber Command was thrown at such a small target.

35

US troops inspect a captured Me262 jet fighter during the closing days of the war.

German jets

The Messerschmitt Me262 jet fighter had been under development since 1938. It went into service in April 1944. Together with the accident-prone rocket-propelled Me163 Komet, it was by far the fastest fighter aircraft in the closing stages of the war. Its top speed of 870kph was about 160kph faster than the Allies' jet fighter, the British Gloster Meteor, which entered service at the same time. The impact made by the Me262 was limited by Hitler's initial orders for it to be used as a bomber. In its fighter role it inflicted heavy damage on Allied bombers, but it was too late and too few in numbers to change the course of the war.

Nevertheless, by the autumn of 1944 the V-1 menace had been mastered. Massed on the south coast and the approaches to London were anti-aircraft guns firing shells armed with proximity fuses, which exploded near their targets. Fast fighter aircraft, including the newly introduced Gloster Meteor jet, shot down the V-1s at close range or nudged them off course. On 28 August 1944 the defences brought down 90 of the 98 V-1s that approached or crossed Britain's coastline. By the beginning of September 1944 the worst of the V-1 offensive was over. The V-1 launching sites in northern France had been captured by the advancing Allies, forcing the Germans to fire the doodlebugs at longer range from Holland or from converted bombers flying over the North Sea.

Anti-aircraft batteries on the south coast of Britain wait for the V-1s. Of the 9,000 V-1s fired at Britain from mid-June to mid-September 1944, about 3,600 were shot down by guns and aircraft.

There was no relief for Londoners. On 8 September the first V-2 rocket, fired only minutes before from a site in Holland, fell on the London suburb of Chiswick with an explosion which could be heard all over the city. Rumours quickly spread that the explosions were caused by gas mains catching fire. The government, fearing mass panic if it told the public about this new terror weapon, did not reveal the V-2's existence until November 1944.

The V-2 rocket, which could carry a tonne of explosives over a range of 320 kilometres. Each V-2 was at least 20 times more expensive for the Germans to produce than a V-1.

Unlike the V-1, the V-2 gave no warning of its approach and could not be intercepted after it had been launched. It climbed about 100 kilometres before hurtling to earth at up to four times the speed of sound. Transported on a vehicle that was also its launcher, it could be fired from almost any level piece of ground. Its launching sites were constantly changed to avoid detection from the air.

The V-2 offensive reached a climax in February 1945, during which 232 fell on southern England. One of the worst V-2 incidents occurred shortly afterwards, on 8 March, when a rocket fell on London's Smithfield Market on a busy morning, killing 233 people. In all, 1,115 V-2s fell on England, 517 of them in the London area. Over 1,000 V-2s were also fired at the Belgian port of Antwerp, in an attempt to deny the Allies the use of its harbour during the closing months of the war.

On 27 March 1945 the last V-2 to reach England exploded at Orpington in Kent. Two days later the last V-1 to get through Britain's defences fell to earth near Hatfield, 30 kilometres from London. The V-weapons killed nearly 9,000 people in Britain and seriously injured another 25,000. They had given the British a nasty few months and had forced the Allies to devote considerable resources to dealing with them But none of this had halted the build-up of Allied forces in northern Europe, which sealed Germany's fate. Nor had the V-weapons broken the morale of the British civilians in the firing line.

The V-weapons did not alter the course of the war but they did point the way to the future. The V-1 was the ancestor of the cruise missiles that were fired against Iraq during the Gulf War in 1991. The V-2 was the forerunner of the mobile ballistic missiles that in the 1970s became mainstays of the US and Soviet nuclear arsenals. At the end of the war the V-2's designer, Wernher von Braun, was captured by the Americans. He was taken to the USA where he played an important part in the research that put satellites in space and men on the Moon.

Wernher von Braun, who had been a rocket scientist for the Nazis during the war, with a model of the Venus probe he designed in the USA for the government in the late 1950s.

The atomic bomb race

At dawn on 16 July 1945 a colossal fireball burst over the New Mexico Desert, fusing the sand to glass and exploding with a force equivalent to 20,000 tonnes of TNT. Immediately afterwards a mushroom cloud boiled up 12,000m into the sky. With the testing of the first atomic bomb, a new era in warfare had dawned.

In 1934 the physicist Leo Szilard, a Hungarian-born Jewish refugee from Nazi Germany, discovered that the nuclei of certain atoms could be split by bombarding them with atomic particles known as neutrons. In turn this would release more neutrons, which would split more nuclei, and so on in a chain reaction releasing huge amounts of energy.

Scientists realized that the energy could be used to create a bomb of enormous power. In Britain two more refugees from Nazi Germany, Otto Frisch and Rudolf Peierls, found that a rare form of uranium, uranium-235, was required to produce an instantaneous explosive chain reaction of the type required for a bomb. Meanwhile physicists working in France discovered that an artificial element, plutonium, could also be used to make an atomic bomb.

A mushroom cloud rises 20,000 feet over the Japanese city of Nagasaki after the explosion of the second atom bomb in the city on 9 August 1945.

39

Atomic research was also well advanced in Germany. Many scientists were fearful of the consequences of an atomic weapon being placed in the hands of the German leader, Adolf Hitler. In 1939 in the USA, Albert Einstein, the leading physicist of the day and another refugee from Nazi Germany, warned President Roosevelt that Germany might be planning to build an atomic weapon. Prompted by Szilard, Einstein proposed an American research project to develop an atomic bomb. He also wrote that the bomb should never be used.

Roosevelt responded by setting up a Uranium Committee, which reported in July 1941 that it would be possible to design and build an atomic bomb.

Albert Einstein – the brilliant scientist – takes the oath of US citizenship in 1940. A year earlier he had warned President Roosevelt of the danger of an atomic weapon in the hands of the German leader Adolf Hitler. Einstein was a Jewish refugee from Hitler's anti-Jewish laws.

Chillingly, the Committee concluded that in any future war the use of such a weapon would be 'determining'.

Meanwhile the British were also working on a nuclear weapons project, codenamed Tube Alloys.

The pace quickened when the United States entered the war after the Japanese attack on Pearl Harbor on 7 December 1941. The British scientific team joined forces with the Americans in the race to beat Germany to the atomic bomb. Joint research was transferred to the USA under the codename Manhattan Project. Many of the Allies' most brilliant brains were gathered together in a specially built laboratory complex at Los Alamos, New Mexico.

In the summer of 1945, after two billion dollars had been spent, a plutonium bomb was ready for testing.

Scientists from the Manhattan Project measure radioactivity in the ground after the explosion of the first atom bomb at Alamogordo in New Mexico. The man with the hat is Robert Oppenheimer, the scientific director of the project. By 1945 about 125,000 people were working on the top secret Manhattan Project. Uranium-235 was produced at a huge plant at Oak Ridge, Tennessee which covered 200 square kilometres. Plutonium was made in the nuclear reactors at Hanford in Washington state.

Three weeks later the atomic bomb was used against Japan. On 6 August an American B-29 heavy bomber dropped the uranium-235 version of the bomb, the torpedo-shaped Little Boy, on the city of Hiroshima. Ten square kilometres of its centre were flattened, 78,000 people killed. On 9 August another B-29 dropped Fat Man, a bulbous plutonium bomb, on Nagasaki, where 35,000 died. Japan formally surrendered to the Allies on 2 September. The scientists who created the atomic bomb could not know what they had unleashed, because such a bomb had never been set off before. The effect on the people of Hiroshima was dreadful: *'The moment there was a flash, it felt as if thickly mixed paint was thrown at me, and I thought Heaven had fallen. . . I went into the house though I was scared. the tap water was dripping slowly, so I washed my face there, but I just couldn't get rid of something sticky, and when I pulled it with my hand, the thin skin-like thing stuck and wouldn't come off. . . When we reached the hospital it was packed, and they wouldn't treat us. After three long hours they put mercurochrome on my child but told me that adults should have patience. my chest was burning, my stomach ached like I was in labour, and my eyes became hazy.'*[6]

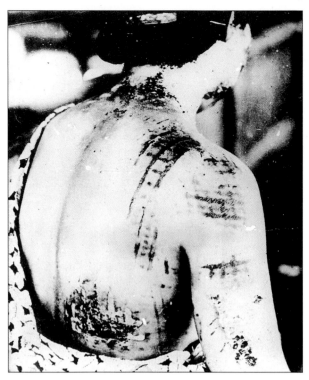

The pattern of a kimono burned on to the back of a victim of the Hiroshima bomb. Over 100,000 Japanese were killed when the atom bombs were dropped on Hiroshima and Nagasaki, and thousands more later died of radiation-linked illnesses. The US president, Harry S Truman, did not hesitate to order the dropping of the bombs: he had been told that an invasion of Japan could cost the Allies a million casualties.

The war in Europe had ended on 8 May 1945, over two months before the testing of the plutonium bomb in New Mexico. After the German surrender the Allied teams investigating Germany's atomic weapons programme found that German research lagged behind the Allies by at least two years. Only one atomic reactor had been built, and this had not begun to produce material for a bomb.

From the start German atomic research had been mismanaged. The Nazis' persecution of the Jews in the 1930s had forced many of the most talented Jewish scientists to emigrate to Britain and the United States, where they later joined the Manhattan Project. In the early part of the war German scientific and technical research concentrated on achieving quick results at the expense of investment in longer-term projects. The work that was started on atomic weapons was disrupted by continual power struggles within the Nazi Party which delayed research and development in all scientific and technical fields. At one point there were 12 separate teams competing with each other to present Adolf Hitler with an atomic bomb. Hitler, however, placed little faith in nuclear physics, preferring to encourage the development of rockets and jets, which he mistakenly regarded as the weapons which would turn the tide of the war.

The Allies also succeeded in sabotaging Germany's only heavy water plant, in occupied Norway. The increasing ferocity of the bombing campaign against Germany itself disrupted the efforts of the atomic scientists. Finally, it has been suggested that some of Germany's leading physicists, unhappy about the prospect of handing Hitler an atomic bomb, deliberately delayed the programme.

Medicine at war

Medical science made great strides during the Second World War. The storage of blood by the separation of its plasma from the red corpuscles reduced the death toll from wounds. The use of antibiotics, produced in quantity in the USA after the British had devised the methods for doing so, saved tens of thousands of lives. The importance of antibiotics was dramatically demonstrated in the Far East. Here the Allies were able to use suppressive drugs to control endemic disease like malaria. The Japanese had no such drugs. When the last Japanese offensive in Burma collapsed in 1944, the victorious (and immunized) Allied troops discovered that as many Japanese soldiers had died from disease as from wounds.

The terrible burns often suffered in mechanised warfare stimulated new techniques in plastic surgery. The most famous plastic surgeon of the war was the New Zealander, Sir Archibald McIndoe, who worked with pilots who had been badly burned during the Battle of Britain. McIndoe was not only concerned with the repair of his patients' disfigurements but also with their mental recovery and return to normal life. He was responsible for the abolition of the so-called 90-day rule, under which badly injured men were compulsorily invalided out of the service after that period had passed.

A landing craft evacuates wounded US troops from Normandy two weeks after the D-day landings. War produces as many mental scars as physical wounds, and the Second World War saw great advances in the treatment of combat stress.

Conclusion

An advanced German rocket designed at the end of the war. By 1945 the Germans had developed an impressive new generation of rockets, including Wernher von Braun's Wasserfall (waterfall) radio-controlled supersonic guided anti-aircraft missile. This could have destroyed aircraft at a height of 20,000 metres and a range of 70 kilometres. Wasserfall was invented too late to be used in the Second World War.

The Second World War began with a cavalry charge by Polish horse soldiers, and ended six years later with the dropping of an atomic bomb. Among the weapons the Allies found in Germany at the end of the war were many that were the forerunners of today's military arsenals. Among them were delta-wing bombers and variable-geometry jets, helicopters, radio-controlled surface-to-air missiles and wire-guided air-to-air missiles.

German scientists had also produced nerve gases that could be fatal within 15 minutes. Sadly these nerve gases have been used since the end of the war, by the Iraqi dictator Saddam Hussein against the Kurdish people.

Many of the developments of the war years were beneficial later: the mass production of antibiotics; the growing importance of computer technology; and the rockets of the US and Soviet space programmes. But the same rockets that carried astronauts into space have also been designed to carry nuclear weapons. And wartime links between scientists, governments and the armed forces led to massive post-war spending on arms technology, which has done much to distort the economies of small and large nations in the post-war years.

A modern descendant of the V-1, the Tomahawk cruise missile used against Iraq in the Gulf War of 1991.

Timeline

1929 **October 29th** Wall Street Crash, triggers Great Depression.
1931 **April 14th** Spain becomes a republic.
1933 **January 30th** Hitler appointed Chancellor of Germany. **August 2nd** Hitler becomes Fuhrer (German dictator).
1935 **October 2nd** Italian troops invade Ethiopia.
1936 **February** Popular Front wins elections in Spain.
March 8th German troops enter Rhineland.
July 18th Rebellion by Army officers begins Spanish Civil war. **November 1st** Italy and Germany sign Rome-Berlin Axis. **1937 July 7th** Japan attacks China. **November 6th** Italy, Germany and Japan sign the Anti-Comintern Pact.
1938 **March 12th** Anschluss (union of Germany and Austria) declared: German troops occupy Austria.
August-September International confrontation over Hitler's demands for part of Czechoslovakia (the Sudentenland).
September 30th Munich Conference resolves Czech crisis.
October 12th German troops occupy Sudetenland.

1939 **March 12th** German forces occupy Czechoslovakia. **28th** Franco's forces capture Madrid: Spanish civil war ends. **31st** France and Britain guarantee Polish independence.
May 2nd Germany and Italy agree Pact of Steel alliance. **August 23rd** USSR-German non-aggression pact agreed. **September 1st** Germany invades western Poland. **3rd** France and Britain declare war on Germany. **17th** Soviet troops invade eastern Poland.

1940 **April 7th** Norway and Denmark attacked by Germany. **May 10th** German troops begin invasion of Netherlands, Belgium and Luxembourg. Churchill becomes British prime minister. **12th** Germany begins invasion of France.
June 10th Italy declares war on Britain and France. **14th** German forces capture Paris. **22nd** French sign armistice at Compiegne. Battle of Britain begins.
September 27th Germany, Italy and Japan sign the Tripartite Pact. **November 5th** Roosevelt re-elected US president. **14th** Coventry levelled by German bombers.

1941 **March 11th** Lend-Lease Act signed. **April 17th** Germany starts invasion of Balkans and Greece. **June 22nd** Invasion of USSR by Germany (Operation Barbarossa) begins.
July US oil embargoes on oil and steel exports to Japan. **August 14th** Roosevelt and Churchill sign Atlantic Charter, agreeing war aims. **November** German forces halted outside Moscow.

December 7th Japan bombs US naval base at Pearl Harbor, Hawaii. Japan declares war on USA.
8th USA and Britain declare war on Japan. **11th** Germany and Italy declare war on USA: USA declares war on them.

1942 **February 15th** Singapore captured by Japanese. **April 9th** US forces on Bataan Peninsula surrender. **May 6th** US forces on Corregidor surrender. **July** Battle of Stalingrad begins.
November 8th US and British troops land in North Africa. **11th** German forces enter Vichy France.

1943 **January 14-24th** Casablanca Conference agrees Allied war aim of unconditional enemy surrender. **February 2nd** German army at Stalingrad surrenders. **May 12th** War ends in North Africa. **July 10th** Allied forces land in Sicily.
26th Mussolini resigns. **September 3rd** Allies land in Italy. **8th** Italy surrenders. **10th** Nazi forces occupy Rome. **November 22-25th** Cairo Conference.
28th Tehran Conference opens.

1944 **March** Soviet troops enter Poland.
June 4th Allied troops enter Rome.
6th D-day: Allied invasion of France begins. **July 20th** Hitler wounded in assassination attempt by German officers. **21st** Dumbarton Oaks conference lays down basis for United Nations. **August** Warsaw Uprising starts. **25th** Paris liberated. **October** Warsaw Uprising crushed. **6th** Soviet forces enter Hungary and Czechoslovakia. **20th** US forces enter Philippines.
November All-out US bombing of Japan begins.
December 16th German troops attack through Ardennes.

1945 **February 4th** Yalta conference.
April 1st US forces occupy Okinawa.
12th Roosevelt dies: Truman US president. **20th** Soviet forces enter Berlin. **28th** Mussolini executed. **May 1st** Hitler's suicide announced in Berlin. **2nd** Berlin captured. **7th** Germany signs unconditional surrender.
June 26th UN formed. **July 17th** Potsdam conference opens. **August 6th** Atomic bomb dropped on Hiroshima. **8th** Atomic bomb dropped on Nagasaki.
September 2nd Japan signs surrender.

1946 **March 5th** Churchill's 'Iron Curtain' speech.
1947 **March 12th** Truman Doctrine outlined.
June 5th Marshall Plan put forward.
1948 **June 24th** USSR begins blockade of West Berlin (ends May12th 1949)

Glossary

Amphibious operation   A military operation that involves travelling on both water and land. The most famous and largest amphibious operation ever was the Normandy landings of June 1944 - D-Day.

Blind landing system   A system of electronic beacons that enable an aircraft to land at night or in very poor weather conditions.

Breakwater   A solid structure, usually built around a harbour, which breaks the force of the waves.

Cipher   A secret code that can be understood only by those in possession of the key to it.

Cruise missile   A modern type of missile capable of carrying warheads a long distance. Towards the end of the Cold War in the 1980s there were many cruise missiles designed to carry nuclear warheads, the descendants of the nuclear bombs that flattened Hiroshima and Nagasaki at the end of the Second World War.

Fat Man   The atomic bomb that was dropped on the Japanese city of Nagasaki on 9 August, 1945, killing 35,000 people and ending the war.

Flail   A chain or group of chains with a weight mounted on the end: the weights can then be swung at things from a distance. During the Second World War tanks were mounted with flails so that weights could be swung at mines, to detonate them safely.

Heavy water   A vital ingredient in the building of an atomic reactor. Before the fall of France in 1940 the British acquired from the French all the world's supplies of heavy water, to use in their nuclear bomb project 'Tube Alloys'.

Infra red   A type of light present at night. Infra-red glasses can see it, and special types of film pick it up on photographs.

Little Boy   The atomic bomb dropped on Hiroshima in Japan on 6 August, 1945, which killed 78,000 people.

Magic   The codename given to secret information the USA had obtained by breaking Japanese codes.

Milch cow   A cow kept for milking. The German navy used the term to describe the U-boats that carried fuel out to the wolfpacks at sea.

Monoplane   An aircraft that has only one wing on each side of its main body.

Munitions   Military equipment, especially ammunition.

Occupied Europe   The parts of Europe occupied by Germany and its allies during the Second World War, stretching from the west coast of France to Greece and Poland in the east.

Pressurization   The same air pressure inside a container as would normally be felt at ground level. In a pressurized aircraft those on board can move about comfortably at a height where there would not normally be enough air to breathe.

Proximity fuses   Fuses that set off bombs when they were close to the target, instead of when they actually hit it (which had been the case in the past). The famous US general, George Patton, said that 'The new shell with the funny fuse is devastating. . . I think that when all armies get this shell we will have to devise some new method of warfare'. (In *War Winners*, R.W. Clark, Sidgewick and Jackson 1979.)

Reconnaissance   A mission to discover what the enemy is doing.

Ruhr   The industrial region on Germany's western border with France. Although less important now, for the first two-thirds of the twentieth century the Ruhr was the main base of German industry. The Ruhr was occupied by French and Belgian troops in 1923, when Germany failed to pay the reparations it owed as result of the First World War. The troops were only withdrawn two and a half years later, when in October 1925 the border between France and Germany was agreed at the Locarno Conference.

Spanish Civil War   A revolt against the elected government begun in October 1936 by army officers led by General Franco. The army officers were right wing and very conservative; they were worried that the government was too left wing and that it stood against the Catholic church. The war ended when government forces in Madrid surrendered on 28 March 1939, by which time German pilots in Spain had perfected the dive-bombing techniques they later used in the Second World War.

Strategic bombing   Bombing attacks on targets that are specially selected to harm the enemy's ability to wage war: for example, transport networks, factories and the cities in which workers live.

Ultra   The secret information obtained by the British by solving German codes.

U-boat   *Unterseeboot* (underseaboat). U-boats almost won the Battle of the Atlantic for Germany, by cutting Britain's supply routes from North America.

Wolfpacks   The groups of German submarines that hunted together during the Second World War.

Books to read

The Blitz Fiona Reynoldson (Wayland 1990)

Soldier Through History Peter Chrisp (Wayland 1992)

Blitzkrieg Peter Chrisp (Wayland 1990)

The Origins of the Second World War Peter Allen (Wayland 1991)

The Other Ultra: Codes, Ciphers and the Defeat of Japan Ronald Lewin (Hutchinson 1982)

The Rise of Fascism Peter Chrisp: for information on the Spanish Civil War (Wayland 1991)

Ultra Goes to War Ronald Lewin (Hutchinson 1978)

ACKNOWLEDGEMENTS

1 in *The Bombers: Strategy and Tactic* Robin Cross (Bantam 1986); **2** in *The Sunday Telegraph Battle of Britain* ed. Robin Cross (1989); **3** in *The Battle of Hamburg* Martin Middlebrook (Penguin 1980); **4** in *The Battle of the Atlantic* Terry Hughes and John Costello (Collins 1977); **5** in *Unsung Heroines* Robin Cross, Jenny de Gex and Vera Lynn (Sidgewick and Jackson 1990); **6** in *The Atomic Bomb, Voices from Hiroshima and Nagasaki* Kyoto & Mark Seldon (East Gate, 1989).

Index

Pictures accompanied by text are indexed in **bold**.